Bno BL

Please return/renew this item by the last date shown
on this label, or on your self-service receipt.

To renew this item, visit **www.librarieswest.org.uk**
or contact your library.

Your Borrower number and PIN are required.

**LibrariesWest**

4 1 0077301 1

# The Woman
# Who Was Not There

Joelle Taylor

Burning Eye

This edition published by Burning Eye Books 2014

www.burningeye.co.uk

@burningeye

Burning Eye Books

15 West Hill, Portishead, BS20 6LG

ISBN 978 1 90913 639 7

# Contents

# Foreword

Joelle observes the reality of modern-day life, pinpoints the absurdities and the injustices, and then reminds us that we are human, and that sometimes the best way to make sense of it is through poetry. The thing I have always liked about Joelle's poetry is that it has guts, it has rhythm, and it has attitude. The thing I like about this collection is that it continues that tradition.

In these times of austerity, hypocrisy, political corruption, and mindless reality television, we need poetry like this. Joelle Taylor does not mess about. Her poetry is fearless. It gets right to the point.

Her poetry has purpose.

Benjamin Zephaniah

# Preface

Imagine this page is an empty theatre. No one has arrived yet. A poet stands in the centre of a deserted stage. She talks into a microphone that will collect all of her words and add them to the thousands of other voices kept safe within it. The ancestral poets are a part of her poem. They add a line. Take out a word. If you tip your ear to the head of the microphone just before a set begins you can hear them whisper across the centuries. Eventually someone walks in and takes a seat. They listen. And now the poem is complete.

These poems were written quietly with my tongue. They are meant to be spoken. Mainly to yourself.

Words change worlds. There can be no doubt about that. Poetry turns every wound into a mouth. Words create worlds. I spend my life these days reminding the young and ill-fitting that a pen is the needle point on a compass. Follow it. Your pen always knows the way home.

All poetry is dangerous. Some of it leaps out of the darkness at you. Some poems are slow-acting but equally lethal. You will find that some poems even follow you home. These poems have followed me since I was a child. While most were written in the last couple of years, they have been watching me from street corners and out of the edges of their eyes for years – from tower block windows, peering through the flaps of ill-conceived shelters at Greenham Common, across the stormy white tundra of chill-outs, through darkened dance floors before finally waiting for me at the crossroads of the dressing room, the stage, and the quiet space at the back of the house. There is a fourth turning, but I try not to go down that one.

There are town centres and council estates pressed between these pages like concrete butterflies. There are women who eat themselves and girls whose songs tear the world in two. There are pregnant men, and women who keep their souls in jars on high shelves or lovers hung in neat rows in wardrobes. There are advent calendars of tower blocks with sharp-toothed stories concealed where the chocolates should be. Women write themselves and children tap-dance in the centre of light bulbs. There is poetry tattooed on the side of tenement buildings and graffitied across skin. There are women who are not there.

Some of the poems you will not understand. This does not matter. Some of the best poems are written in invisible ink. Some of the best conversations are unspoken.

Every one of these poems is about freedom of speech. Every one of these poems understands the limits of its page, and that bars across our exercise books translate to bars across prison cells for some writers across the world. We are each cultural revolutionaries, and each of us has the potential to use our words to create something better, something beautiful. Even as I write this sentence the world changes. Stretches its wings.

Even this full stop is a tiny mouth. Listen.

Yesterday, upon the stair,
I met a man who was not there.
He was not there again today.
I wish, I wish he'd go away.

*William Hughes Mearns*


When they throw you to the lions,
return wearing a fur coat.

*Kareem Parkins-Brown*

for the three of us

# The Last Poet Standing

**(I)**

I am the last poet standing
on this blank stage
of bruised pavements,
broken with missed opportunities
and well-aimed misunderstandings.
They say our children are too demanding.
The scent of sweat at the base of the spine
carried on wolves of wind
lures the gangs in.

Even the air we breathe has chalk lines around it;
police barrier tape surrounds it
while the skin of our streets
is tattooed with grin and gut graffiti,
the city's obituary
cut by street artists, cultural terrorists and infant infantry,
sprayed in blood and ink

Our young are force-fed on vulnerability and violence.
Their lullabies are the cries of police sirens
and the echo of doors slamming late under midnight moons as
    wide as children's eyes.
She didn't come home again tonight.
She never will.
But that child
will wait for her for the rest of his life.

**(II)**

These canals, these tracks, these umbilical streets,
these arteries of our cities
are clogged with discarded dreams and shopping trolleys.

Our kids die in school corridors,
not just in intangible, illegal, immoral wars
but the simpler war between
self-respect and self-esteem.

Children,

on these roads it is expected that you will stumble fumble
   HUMBLE your grip on your dream –
but they are the only things we have,
these delusions of equality.
So stand up, speak free, exercise linguistic liberty,
*shut up and speak*
because disappointment is viral
to the point where low expectation equals survival
and when there is little sense of truth, honour and justice
it is tempting to become tribal.

**(III)**

Our thin children have dug themselves in to their own fragile skin
and hide behind sandbags, strips of colour, postcodes and lies
and a cheap pound shop pride
and a knife.
Always a knife –
that reflects the hand that holds it;
the blade reflects the hand that holds it.

When you see your face
can you remember your name?

Our fathers are pugilist or foetal,
boxers or babies,
missing in action,
a paste link in the cheap chain reaction
that leaves us lost in our own living rooms
and he,
he is just an empty chair, an empty promise
or the hierarchy of the fist above the kiss,
a shadow receding in the mist,
retreating in the mist.

Fear is your father forgetting your name.

It's getting dark.
We are a long way from home
and from a distance
that drained and greying tower block
is a gravestone
and every window lit is a word upon it.
But who will write our epitaphs when all the poets have gone?
Who will write our epitaphs when all the poets have gone?
Who is going to write our epitaphs when all the young poets have
    gone?

We will never rest in peace –
not while police stand guard outside school gates
and children have Kentucky fried complexions
and education is dependent upon government inspection
and knowledge is privilege
and the libraries of our lives are pillaged.

We will never rest in peace –
not while children cannot spell their own names
and they are the monsters beneath their own beds
and they're afraid of themselves and everything they wish they'd
  said
and the colour of ink is red
and this whole town is proof-marked in blood.

Not while there is one poet left standing.

**(IV)**

We have been worshipping false prophets for false profits:
the cult of celebrity,
the cynical, cyclical celebration of hypocrisy
that allows us to watch the outside world as though it is reality TV
while our children are outside
bent-kneed
picking broken glass from their eyes,
broken class.
You see,
there was never an end to slavery.
We just don't define it anymore simply by ethnicity
but by economy.
Can you hear the gangs howling
from the plains of Peckham to the hard lands of Hackney?

They have your scent.

**(VI)**

You will see me.
You will see poetry
written among the broken glass and the graffiti,
starring in the shattered lenses of CCTV.

You will see poetry.

You will see poetry
in the Braille of night skies,
in the length of time a parent takes to say goodbye,
son, see you soon,
in the harvest moon of children's eyes
or that girl perched on the lip of the tower block preparing to fly
as wild birds escape the gilded bars of her ornamental rib cage,
even in the ganglands' wasteland warrior cries.

Every one of these tower blocks is a book.
Open it.
There is hope in it.

There is poetry.

# No Man's Land

His face was a foreign country
and his tongue was a concealed gun.
His laugh was an air raid siren
and his mouth a deep cave dug in Iraqi earth,
a shallow grave on the edge of town.
His beard was the barbed-wire fence that surrounded the camp
and his skin was a hand-written map sewn into his shirt,
a deserted field at midnight.
His eyes were abandoned soft buried landmines
and his voice was radio static caught between stations.
His ribs were the gripped bars of a Guantanamo Bay cage
and his lips the careful line at Customs,
the border between territories.

And he walked like a school child lost in the rubble of her home
and he spoke like a low-flying plane looking to land.
Welcome to England.
Asalaam alaikum.

But Immigration Central was a love letter written in another
    language
and when he smiled
his teeth
were the New York
skyline.

# The Children

*For the young carers of Skye.*

There are children
who sleep in school uniform,
whose ties
are untidy umbilical cords
that link them
to the woman upstairs with the bad cough
that sounds like someone's digging
and the eyes that never close.

All night, she digs.

There are children
whose blazers are finger-printed,
whose skirts are silent,
whose smiles are stained
as they arrive late to the school gate
again.

*Sorry, miss. Sorry, sir. The dog ate the bus. The bus ate my mother and*
*my mother ate my father*
*and my father ate me.*
*No, I don't know him*
*but I am told*
*that I am just. Like. Him.*
*If you lean closer*
*you can see the space where he used to be.*

An overturned chair.
A cup that no one drinks from.

Some children

wash themselves inexpertly
in the water of their mother's constant self-pity
or the spittle of the shouting man.
Some children leave their skin in the washing machine
too long
on too high a temperature
until it no longer fits them.

There are children
who sleep in school uniform
and dream
of a night without dreams.

# International Pen Pal

*It is strange to think that everything I write or perform and every positive workshop I lead will be taxed and that money transformed into weapons of war. An estimated 17,400 civilians have been killed since the war in Afghanistan began. I will work with the refugees of that war, and will be taxed per poem I help create and write myself. That tax will be used to create more refugees of war who I will then go and work with.*

This poem is a bullet.

Each hammered word
the march of boots.
Each strike of type
a semi-automatic rattle.
I have written armies;
do not listen to me.

This poem is friendly fire.

This poem is
the shifting of the earth,
the assassin that sleeps beneath her feet
as she leaves early that day to collect thin firewood
that when lit will keep her family cold for centuries.
This poem has waited years
and when it speaks,
opens its red mouth,
the whole world falls to its knees and weeps.

She is an explosion wrapped in ribbon.
May I be forgiven.

This poem is a young man
uprooted from Customs

and potted in a tight airless room
before men
with tight airless smiles
and asked to spell his name
again,
spell it again.
This poem is a passport
torn in two,
stamped
with boot marks.

This poem is a young girl
in burkha and Nike
hiding beneath a bus seat
as strange-dressed men come
and pick off the women one by one,
sniper smiles held to their heads
as soldiers look to the whispering men to speak;
this poem is the last thing she reads.

This poem has taken language;
each word written here has scrubbed out a mother tongue.
This poem has eaten history.
This poem is history.
This poem lies silent beneath dusty roads
or waits at the outskirts of woods
or bursts into a house at 3am
sobbing through oiled shotgun-barrel eyes
with mouths of mass graves.
This poem has lined relatives up against walls
and told them to dance.

Dance.

This poem wants to be a roof,
it wants to be wood,
a school desk,
a bus seat.
It wants to be the correct spelling of a name,
a sleeping relative,
silence.

This poem wants to be a poem

but

this poem is a bullet.
A real poet would not write it.

# The Man Who Ironed Butterflies

Once upon a tick of heels,
a shiver of loose change,
there was a child trapped beneath the ice of a full-length mirror.

Earlier that night
if you remember
was the laying out of ties,
each gently draped around an arm as thick as my waist,
as dialect,
my smile – as polished as promises –
reflected in your cufflinks
as you cut away your face
and left embryos of curled hair clogging the plug hole,
my brothers and sisters.
The air was aftershave and alcohol.
I sewed a suit from it as you left.

Later
I woke,
my dreams punched flat as vowels,
and heard the sound of you
walking in my mother's shoes on the curled-lip lino of her room.
I stood at the edge of the stairs
and stared.

You,
rolled shirt sleeves,
plaid forgotten family tartan,
working men's genes
in the rolling mist of the kitchen
that seemed

to form the faces of our ancestors,
dark outside,
a winter yellow dawn within,
a light bulb somewhere swung
and you

you

stretched over the board
dragon in hand,
loosened tie,

ironing butterflies.

I stood in the doorway. Spilt words. Stupid girl.

This was men's work. These were working men's dreams.

You laid each butterfly out
softly,
carefully,
wings spread and pinned
like children before dressing,
and steamed
perfect creases down the centre of each.
The pile to your left grew
and I knew, sir, I knew
that I would grow to be a better man than you.

You have made the natural world neat,
sir.
Gardens grow in squares
in perfect parentheses,

birds follow precise flight paths
and your daughter trims her skin nightly.

I want to wake up ugly
and I do. I do.

I cannot fit back into my cocoon,

this body that would not fit,
this suit sewn of strange men's skin,
this tie that became my tongue,
this shirt I lost my way in.

I shave my face to find you.
You are buried there,
a child beneath ice
beneath a full-length mirror.
I remember

alone. A slow waltz on the tip of my tongue.
Dancing in dead men's skins.

I dress as you while you are sleeping.
I dress as you while I am sleeping.

# Crystal Kisses

## (I)

Girls at the top
of ivory tower blocks:
cut
your hair.

Your bandanaed Pimp Charming will not save you.
He has already betrayed you;
he is not climbing but pulling.
These are not your dreams he is fulfilling
as he stands before you half-drunk, grinning,
introducing you to the gang,
this half-boy scrubbed-out man,
and it's all part of a long written subtextual plan
that once seemed like a love letter
in invisible ink.
But this boy has been patient,
two hands on her window ledge
and in one an invitation to the group initiation
he forgot to mention.

He makes her presents of stealing gifts.
She is bowed in the presence of crystal kisses.
Pass the parcel.
Delicate and vicious,
they surround her in the disused lift.
No poetry. No pity.
Their eyes the blank windows of a somnambulant city
as her name is spray-tagged in urinal graffiti.
They circle her.

One winks. Offers a drink
and their shoulder blades are shark fins,
these awkward angry boys
all angles and apologies
with blue siren voices
that she once shared a classroom with.
Their tongues are now whips
that scar her unwritten skin
into a map,
each word, each wound
a passport mark of origin
that confines her to the estate.
*Know your place.*
She may not wear a burkha
but there is more than one form of purdha;
she wears her hair across her face like crime scene tape.

And I have learned not to look
at these boys with mouths of burning books,
and I head quietly back to my flat.
Doors close like eyes will. All is still. All is still.

**(II)**

Down the catwalk gangways
she teaches herself to walk. One foot. Two foot.
And the air she moves through
is forever outlined in chalk.
She walks
back bruised by the beating of the communal metal bins
they forced her in,
back bruised by the looks of other women
clutching six packs of children

pre-school mewling
as she carefully, warily passes by;
the girls on this block
wear half-drawn net curtains across their eyes,
but she will learn like the rest to bury her breasts in the shallow
grave of her chest.
A sunken spine will always offer more protection in these ends
than a Kevlar vest.

## (III)

They tell you not to join a gang
but not that you will grow up in one,
that these are your friends,
these razor-mouthed men,
not that those same boys who once dealt Pokémon in the
playground
are now shotting crack and blow and smack and snow
on indifferent street corners
in the less curious parts of town,
frightened and furious,
kissing fists,
boy soldier street existentialists
pressing stealing gifts
on to well-dressed strangers with wet upper lips,
a storm in the centre of their palms.
Do not speak to her about self-harm.
If this was Iran
she would be stoned to death for what they did to her,
but this is Hackney
so she just gets stoned.

Those same boys who once played kiss chase

now play kiss chase
and the moon hides its face in the branches of a tree.

## (IV)

The girls that are locked in ivory tower blocks
around these ends
are kept well-fed and confined to their beds
like battery hens
stored one on top of the other
like an Argos advent calendar.
Pop the windows.
Inside a girl grows into a woman into a widow
and grieves the girl.

There are parts of her body,
places where even the police won't go,
cordoned-off skin where the grass will not grow
in the dark heart of the tower block shadow
that turns the estate into a sundial.
There are parts of her body that are wastelands and warzones
on which a girl child stands alone
wondering which could be the path that will lead her home
but sensing blood pulls up her hood and sets off quietly into the
    woods
sprayed with their collective pheromones.

## (V)

And when she smiles
her teeth are a white picket fence,
neglected, paint peeling,
that a bouquet of flowers rests against
and nothing sings. Nothing ever sings. Listen.

Nothing tastes as good as that which is forbidden.
Nothing is as public as that which must be hidden,
as impossible and irreverent as the possibility of forgiving.
So where are the cheap flowers resting on railings
for these young falling women?

Where are the T-shirts and the TV appeals,
the parliamentary petitions?
There is just confinement to the tenement as though men are the
    victims
and the female form once again becomes a kind of prison.

**(VI)**

Gang gods battle gods
in a raw estate *Oresteia*
and she is Cassandra,
foreseeing the future
but fated never to be believed,
especially by herself,
who only knows what she thinks by following Facebook news
    feeds.
So the media
call her the all-devouring mother,
Bedsit Medea,
print headlines in graveyard script
and never tell the story of the girl on the twelfth storey
entombed in this family crypt.

But this girl. This girl,
this municipal miracle,
this council estate oracle,
within each iris

33

the globe of a thin world.
She is the universe contained in a single pixel,
the rainbow rising out of the oil spill.

Girls: know your power.

Girls at the top
of ivory tower blocks:
cut your hair.

And when you have and when you do,
tell them
it's because you don't need anyone
to save you.

# Hummingbird

Her heart
was a hummingbird.

It was at about this time
every evening these days
that she would feel the
chest twitch,
smell strange blossoms,
a baroque breeze of music
and know her heart was a

hummingbird.

She carried on for a while.
Smiled,
sipped warm wine between clenched teeth,
discussed endings to books not yet begun,
knowing that her ribs
were a gilded bird cage
and that the beat of its wings
was a hurricane within.
She lay awake
listening
to the sounds of her own
listening,
the flutter and the futility,
this aviary in her chest,
sometimes
a cracked song.

Even birds can forget the words to their songs.

She fed it indifference through the bars,
left seeds,
a plastic mirror,
a bell,
until eventually
after an evening spent dreaming that she would never dream
    again
she awoke

inside a gilded cage
in the chest of a
hummingbird.

Listen to your heart speak.
The Morse code beat.

# The Woman Who Was Not There

It was the summer of '81
when my invisible friend began ignoring me,
turned her back
and stopped speaking,
muttering occasionally from between lips as thin as promises
as notes passed between children,
and refused to take her place at the table beside me
or curl at the bottom of the bed,
sentry and silent.

*What's wrong?* I said.
Years passed as I waited for a reply.

The uncertainty.
After a while I was no longer sure which of us was imaginary.

Outside
clouds of black flies
wrote my name in the air between us
and still I could not spell it.
Sometimes
they drew her face
but it never looked at me.

She was not there
when I opened the back door
and crawled
smile like a fault line
beneath the bed;

she is not there still,
rocking quietly in the corner
singing songs my mother knew.

# The Hunger Striker

**(I)**

Men guard their food when she enters the room.

Her body grew up around her
like a bad neighbourhood,
a natural disaster
in a non-English-speaking country,
no planning permission,
no notice in the post office,
flesh
flood.

Fat.
Female.

Men guard their food when she enters the room.

Here she comes,
rolling like a Southern vowel,
stamping like a syllable.
The Fat. Female.
rode herself
bare-backed into battle.

She ducks the digs
and the last dregs of schoolboy sarcasm
slung over the desk tops,
sentences trimmed
and semi-skimmed.

No matter.

The Fat. Female.
licks her lips,
smiles and sits.
She is
thick-skinned.

But

all of the words thrown
grenade heart
stuck to her bones
in curves of cat
and hold-me-hards.
She is wearing all of the women she would have been,
draped soft and satisfied around her skin,
each character a costume.

Fat. Female.

## (II)

Each fold of fat has a name.
This one is called:
Anna.
Five foot six
of suck my fictional—
Spells her name backwards sometimes
just to avoid being pinned down,
just to avoid being
labelled, pickled, Anna-tated.
Anna is
uncomplicated.

She wears her hair like a hangover,
uses the spare tyre around her waist
to seal her Harley wheels.
See,
here everything has a function,
even eating between meals.

Eating
between mouthfuls.

Speaking
between sentences.

Anna is uneven and ill-fitting
and I suppose that is the attraction.
At least
she never had any problems
in that particular direction.
But.
Right now.
She is taking a slow semi-colon
resting between relationships.
She has
Other Things
on her mind.
Like that bike she forgot to build,
that bad kiss of a poem she fell out with,
that conversation she dropped
back there in the street somewhere
and never quite found again.

Anna
erects her home

hewn from her big bones.
Foundation stone thighs,
fixtures and fittings supplied.
Unbuckles her spine
like a Venetian blind.
Changes the locks.
Breaks into herself.
Squats.
Oh yes,
Anna makes a home
of her big bones.

Men guard their food when she enters the room.

**(III)**

This one is called

Skinny Bitch.
Skim of a thing.
One of those girls you can see all the way around.
Thin as an afterthought.
Pale as a perhaps.
Brittle as friendships.
All angles and apologies
and tight skinny hair
down to her shark-fin hips.

She was weightless.
Whippet.

She had always worn the same pair of heels
on the same pair of shoes.
She did not so much walk

as split the day in two.

The Skinny Bitch
had an elbow in the gut of life,
a boyfriend for every break time,
a flicker book of faces
pressed between the pages of her BlackBerry Filofax
and a silo of sandwiches
emaciated in thinned polythene sacks,
pressed flat
like punched pillows
in the belly of her bag.

She hid food beneath her mattress.
It helped her to sleep.

The Skinny Bitch was popular.
Always eating at Someone Else's house.
Damn,
her mother could hardly remember the last time
she saw her daughter suck up a meal,
and
when was she going to be allowed
to meet this
Someone Else girl
anyway?
The Skinny Bitch
was always eating at
Someone Else's house.
The Skinny Bitch was always
just about to eat.

Funny.

It seemed the more she ate
the less her weight,
seemed the broader and thicker
her thoughts framed
the thinner
she became
almost
as if
she were
eating
herself.

On clear days
you could see straight through her
to who she should have been,
On dense nights
you could trace the geoglyphs of flesh,
the watermarks on her skin.

The Skinny Bitch,
this hunger striker,
rattles the bars to her rib cage,
cuts a record on her stomach of all the meals she has missed –
farmed fresh plough lines,
fences to hold back the thick tide,
sealed lips –
one and two and three and four.
That makes ten
and
begin again.

**(IV)**

Each scratch of skin has a name.
This one is called
Monday.
She holds her stomach in
when she is rutting.
This one is called
Tuesday.
She folds up herself,
trims the waste,
chases the lines
around her face.
This one is
cold;
somebody else stole her skin
when she was not paying attention,
was not looking,
and hung it up to air on the front lawn
next to all the women she wished she had worn.
This one is
cold;
she may never be warm.

**(V)**

Meanwhile.
Back at the cattle ranch.

Fat. Female. has prepared a special meal.
Slips off her skin
as a table napkin,
bones as candelabra,
scapula plates,
and serves herself a meal of white meat and miniskirts.

Rind rump.

Thin slithers of slump.

Her Good Side.

Face.

Neck.

Tongue.

Veal.

Oh yes.

She has prepared herself a special meal.

**(VI)**

The Hunger Striker

rattles the bars to her rib cage;

the Fat. Female.

beats her belly at the cellulite moon

as each eats the thing she loves.

And men?

Men guard their food when they enter the room.

# The Navigator

Keisha
was the kind of girl who left lights on.
Who walked into walls,
spilled her smile down the sulk of her shirt,
stumbled into furniture
like it was her future.

Never did quite fit her body.

Clumsy.

*Keisha!*
*Will you look where you're going?*

Well,
she knew where she was going all right.
Just didn't much appreciate the view.
Did not much appreciate the navigator.
Started to seek alternative routes.

For a clumsy girl
she has a steady hand.

She has sketched a map of herself
on skin stretched tight as fathers' fists,
tracing the long walk home
on the back of her hand,
inner arm,
wrist.

Lines of latitude and longitude.

She scratches herself.
A thirteen-year itch.
She scratches herself.
Thin. Red. Mother. Lips.
Marks against the cell wall,
scratching off the days
until she is sixteen,
when she will draw a thin red line through her skin,
proof marks in the margin of her life,
and she will
begin
again.

Because
when he opened the pages of her blouse like it was a well-read
    book
hardback
he changed the story,
the map,
half-written unedited first draft.
Keisha has her name engraved in guilt
along the stutter of her spine.
*Keisha*
*Volume One*. Underlined.
She is italicised,
a woman walking against the wind.

But listen. Carefully.

When he did that thing

and that thing did her,

Keisha, ceiling clinging,

realised the possibilities

because if he could change the story.

Erase the topography. Eat mountains.

Then. So. Could. She.

Today

Keisha

is the kind of girl who walks upright.

Who walks in spite.

Who carries full friendships in the pockets of her favourite jeans.

Who travels her body like an unexplored land.

Because today

Keisha is the kind of girl who is

a woman.

# Freedom Framed and Hung in the Right Light

You cannot capture freedom.
It cannot be worn around the neck
or mounted on white walls
while we sip warm wine.
It cannot be photographed
or pinned to the pages of a book.
It will not feature on the nightly news
or be cultivated in glass greenhouses
forged from television screens;
that beautiful song you hear
that moves you to tears
is a scream
in a small ornamental bird cage

You cannot capture freedom.
It cannot be balanced on the shoulder
for 40 baht a stroke.
You cannot tell the folks at home
that you held it
and freedom liked it.
It will not stand in doorways
flashing teeth like American Express,
waving hips like colonial flags.

You cannot capture freedom.
You cannot take it home
and clear a space on the mantelpiece.
It will not fit correctly into your suitcase.
It will beat against the sides of the luggage hold

and each of the pounds that shake the aircraft apart
are the final footsteps of its grieving heart
sealed in tin.

You cannot capture freedom.
You cannot ride on its back
or teach it to dance for strangers
or play Connect Four on desolate fairy-lit beaches
while its father watches
and his pocket twitches.

Freedom cannot be captured.

It is wind.
It left before it arrived.
It is the taste you cannot remember.
The art before it becomes
art.
The idea of a song.
The thing before it is named.
The wet ink.

Freedom cannot be captured
and held behind the bars of a page.
Freedom has no home.
You cannot capture freedom
even
in a poem.

# Mosquito Bites

**(I)**

Each dusk
we are haunted by mosquitoes
who dip their beaks
in wells of blood
and each evening
they are hunted by mosquitoes
who dip their beaks
in wells of native women.

It is possible to die from
mosquito
bites

.

**(II)**

When she squashed it against the white wall
to stop its incessant
whine and mutter
it left a red stain
the shape of Thailand
formed from her blood.
Getting closer,
she heard it offer money
and shining things
that looked like stars
but were pieces of silver.

It is difficult to kill things
that have never lived.

**(III)**

The sticky white mosquitoes
with pale hanging bellies
and aging skin
like maps folded into beach bag pockets
swarmed across the land,
clouding around the doorways to bars
and school yards.

They sucked from the youngest first
and then the female
and laid their eggs
in the minds of men,
infecting their bloodstreams
and thickening rivers
with glittering litter,
gaudy hotels,
music without melody
and dancing until feet become
bloody.
And massages
like foetal fist punches.
And kisses
like invading countries.
And thank-yous
like forget-yous.
And pancakes,
cocaine shakes,
construction
like earthquakes.

They say a mosquito
has no soul,
but it does. It does.

It has yours.

# Stylus

She was a quiet cameo of her father,
a tribute in skinny blue sharkskin suit
and knitted tie,
sometimes
an Eton stripe,
a secondary modern sneer.
She styled her hair out of shadows and the corners of rooms,
out of 1979 and the itch of guitars,
smoke from the ghost of his cigarette
and dropped compliments
that clattered clumsy to the floor,
that kitchen lino with the Presley curl.
She wore her heart on the sleeve of an old LP.

Earlier
she shaved in the reflection of his
black Chelsea boots.
Polished them so hard she erased her reflection.
Rubbed herself right out
and re-drew herself in spittle
and the right hairspray.

She dresses as him sometimes
now.
She still carries a straight comb in her inside pocket,
will always do so.
It is a kind of photograph for those who cannot bear to see their
    likeness.
But he lives in her face.
He has to live somewhere.

He does not call
or answer letters
or meet eyes at funerals.

She is a better man than him.

The full-length mirror on the back of the bathroom door
still has her young reflection trapped beneath,
a man tapping on the underside of ice.

Pity
those fathers whose daughters are men
much
much
better than them.

# All That Remains

*You have your mother's mouth,*
he said,
and I wondered how he knew
and whether he suspected I had your ears too;
the truth is
I have a third of you
divided carefully,
equally like we could not manage as children,
cradled in a box your youngest bought
to house all that remains
of our house.

We cried the way men do. The way fields are watered. The way
    clothes are cleaned.

I have my mother's mouth,
her gap that was a gate children ran through,
a smile that we slammed carelessly behind us,
her laugh
as dirty and deep as the grave,
her hands
that fly of their own accord,
that are the birds she kept in the back garden
with promises.

I have my mother's eyes
and finally now
I see me.

# Slimming for Beginners

Her stomach ate her.

Slowly.

Chewed each mouthful carefully.
Did not speak
until it had swallowed her
whole.
Then
finally
it wiped its lips on the crisp white hospice sheets,
smacked them together –
a round of applause,
a maître d' –
and looked at us. Expectant. Pregnant with my mother.

We blinked.
My brother cleared his throat.
I think you might have said something.

It ate us all in the end.
Even this
is written in the dark,
down and deep
in that ectopic stomach
where all our memories sleep.

# Miss Sing

The last time I saw you
I plucked thin petals of cracked glass
from your face,
your still and empty face,
a page before words are dropped into it.

You had been looking in the mirror too long,
had fallen in.

You did not cry.
Not even
when I scrubbed the last of him off you
with wire words,
Dettol
and lies,

not even
when I prised off the fingerprints,
the heart-shaped bruises
from your stuttering skin
so you could not feel him,

not even
when I snapped your tongue
so you could not phone him
and broke your feet
so you could not walk to him
and fitted a fist in each of your ears
so you could not hear him.

You. Did. Not. Cry.

The last time I saw you,
my friend,
my beautiful broken friend,
my scratched diamond,
you were
missing.

# Aims and Ambitions

I learned to shoot as a small girl.
In between
braiding
and
baking
and
brushing away the trail
the men left behind,
dropped promises that rooted in time in the dusty yard,
my mother
named bullets.

This one
is called: Frank.
This one: Uncle Steven. Not a bad man. Not really.
And this: the father who forgot you.

Remember this: you are forgotten.

She taught me to count:
there are six bullets
to a gun barrel,
five fingers to a hand,
two eyes to a tight face
and one finger
for one trigger.

Added all together
it makes
zero.

A hole.

We started
by shooting
washing-up bottles
off the silted kitchen window ledge
and worked our way through
dolls,
beer cans,
unwanted gifts
and lies.

Until finally
she sat me by
my high bedroom window,
kissed my forehead once,
smiled
and together
we watched the men below

scatter

like

minnows.

# Fou Fou

*Fou Fou is a derogatory name for a gay man.*

Maybe
he was thinking of love,
a hand,
or of those eyes
that the west wind blew through,
that were like open windows
he wanted to climb into;

or maybe
he was fingering the phone number
hot
in the parted lips of his pocket
as the dry tongue aromas of Tahir Square
walked beside him,
their lazy arm draped across his shoulder.
*Mujadara.*
*Cumin.*
*Coriander.*
*Vanilla.*
*Salona.*

*Fou. Fou.*

Maybe
he did not understand at first
and the word walked past him
without calling his name.

*Fou Fou,*

they whispered –
a trade wind
bringing strange ships
with black sails –

*Fou. Fou.*
Woman.

Maybe
he thought they wanted a light
for the cigarettes they did not hold
and bent softly
toward the men,
one eyebrow raised
like the velvet curtain
in the forbidden theatre
that crouched in the smiling shadows of the alleyway;

maybe
he heard the night birds serenade him
with illicit melodies
in broken tongues,
and maybe the moon was a mirror ball
and maybe for a while
he thought they were dancing
a slow
silent
waltz,
cheek to cheek,
foot to stomach,
finger to eye;

maybe

he thought he was lying in Hassan's bed still
as they stripped off his clothes
and unpeeled his skin
like a bride's dress
and pulled off his limbs
like an ill-fitting wedding ring
and threw him
tangled in the dusty earth,
a red Rorschach for birds to read.

But maybe
those birds spiralled around his quietened body
like black confetti
before gathering his thin bones
reverently
in their beaks
and scattering them across the desert
to take root in partisan soil;

and maybe
from his thighs,
his femur,
his chipped elbow,
maybe,
just maybe
a thousand more Fou Fou
will grow.

# The Girl Who Was a Book of Poems

She writes poetry on her arms,
on the soft white pages of her body
with nibs of glass
as broken as her home;
she inscribes skin
with the sharp edge of the shadow man's smile,
with the heel of a shoe she wishes she had not worn,
with a shattered baby rattle,
a brittle word,
the thin silhouette that penetrates her curtain in summer,
the crack in the pavement,
the cut of a kiss.

Her arms are archives,
hieroglyphics
it will take centuries to interpret,
her skin
a palimpsest,
words rising from deep below the surface
in red the colour of proof marks
and last night.

She is well edited.
Well read.

And I say nothing
as though that will heal her,
as though silence were a bandage.

I say nothing
as though it were a poem.

# To Understand the Seed Is to Understand the Forest

And within this seed: a tree. Paper. A book. A dusk-lit library.
And within this library: a child. A plan of the town. The folding of
    a torn page. A paper plane
that launches through the window of the library
and out over the marshes into the longest market,
past armies of stalls selling neurotic fruits and strange vegetables.
Faces rise from the concrete like slowly developing photographs;
two children laugh and point at the plane
as it passes tower blocks of Babel where discordant tribes find
    harmony
in the common language of love. Of community.
Gujarati. Hindi. Patois. Yoruba. Cockney.
And at the underground a boy nods to invisible sounds,
a woman waits for herself,
a man bricks his eyes up as promises collect
in the open belly of a basket
and smokers watch ancestors rise from the lit end of cigarettes
while wild teenagers cultivated on street corners finally burst into
    flowers,
one tied to a railing, another given to a single mother.
On Hoe Street a woman irons her smile to wear next Sunday,
hangs love letters on the line to dry, beside fluttering film negatives
    and a greyhound that no longer needs to run. It has arrived.
The plane's shadow traces the rusting vertebrae of the old railway
and on over churches and mosques, temples and synagogues,
the new art of old learning, modern primitives
tending council housing risen from the centre of the village, we
    are contemporary vintage.

Below
the town is writing itself;
those small ink scribbles are smudged lines of people
and gardens exist in parenthesis.
Well-armed neighbours dig front lines on front lawns
in the battle against aphids, the war of the roses,
and still the paper plane noses
through Vinegar Alley, past sunken plague pits,
level with elegant graffiti that spreads as urban ivy,
through the legs of diners on Orford Road and on she goes, into
    Wood Street where collectors grow from the roots of trees,
knowing William Morris watches from the walls of terraced
    houses and every living room is a gallery,
until finally it dives through the letterbox of number 3, to rest on
    the desk of my home.
I unfold the plane, plant seeds in the furrow of my brow

and write this poem.

# Shibboleth

*Shibboleth: a word my enemy is unable to say.*

Shibboleth.
Say it.
My enemy.
My smashed glass.
Say it.

Tonight
I bite.

Shibboleth.
For the thin edge of night.
For 4am.
For the echo of footsteps down dark country veins.
For eyes that speak.
For the silence that follows.
Shibboleth.
For mouths of sand,
forgotten tomorrows.

Shibboleth.
God is dead.
Shibboleth.
I am God.
Shibboleth.
For the shadow buriers.
Shibboleth.
For the invisible tattoo,
that watermark of you.
Shibboleth.

For my dog skin,
restless and uneven.
Shibboleth.
For the house that will not stay still.
For the bright white bitter-sweet pill.
Shibboleth.
For the blank-eye dreams.
For the lost letters.
For the stumble tongue.
For the shy that hid in the corners of my stomach
until shibboleth was sung.

For the forgotten.
For the shame.
For the gilt edged guilt.
For the dropped and cracked name.

Shibboleth.
This secret. This private. This gift. This last breath.
Shibboleth.
For when nothing is left.

# To Dissect a Smile

**(I)**

Her skinny smile
drawn tight as a washing line
was strung with those she had once loved,
swaying,
fluttering
gently on the breeze.
An unposted letter.
The rattle of keys.
The ache of his tread on the gravel path.
A scrawled black cat.
This unopened laugh.

**(II)**

He was an unfinished novel
in a forgotten bottom drawer
when she found him
and brought him
blinking
into the sun,
blew dust from his palimpsest skin,
saw words rising to the surface
but could not read what was written.
And all was well. And all was not.
And the words that are wounds
are best forgot.

**(III)**

She wrote him a son.

Perfect boy.
Man-script.
Hung there beside his father
with eyes of looted shop windows
and his soul a solar eclipse.
He shared his father's face
and pegged his smile in much the same way as her,
although in this light
on this day
his smile was
the sour edge of a razor

**(IV)**

And strung beside the boy
his mother's mother,
worn and neatly folded skin,
the creases indelible
from decades of ironing.
She once pressed her bloodied grin
in the early morning breakfast kitchen
before he came down,
a blunt pulse
and the smile stuck –
now her faded outline
a wind-worn chorus line.

Her smile is a loose thread that snags,
that catches on the heart,
and her face
is a slowly developing
photograph.

**(V)**

Take a cross-section of a smile.
Press it between clear slides.
Place beneath the microscope.
Magnify.
Count the people pegged out
on the smile
to dry.

# The House of Skin

**male order bride**

She kept her other skins
hanging slack in the walk-in wardrobe:
a chorus line of used condoms
or torn tights
from that first treacherous ridiculous night –

when the moon was a rip in fishnets –

each tear is a mouth in the stockings
and they still talk about him now
How they mutter,
little mouths,
and she, head bent,
a heart that flutters
like distant stilettos down dark streets –

she will not listen. Will. Not. Listen.

Damn her. Damn him.
Damn this archive of empty women.

Like the furniture in the low-ceilinged bedroom –
that pressed her
as though between laboratory slides –
the bodies come flat packed,
male order,
foetal in foam,
the instructions either missing

or impossible to read.

She attaches parts with shy feminine brutality.
A smile that is ingrown.
A tease of a hammer.
The forcing of the screw. The coercion.
An arm.
A forehead.
The better part of a leg.

And look. Nothing fits correctly.
The seams will not meet along her thighs.
She cannot fit her own skin.
Bodies do not come in her size.

## (II)

### the changing room

She kept her other skins
hanging slack in the room designated for dressing
like curing bacon
or the tongues of clients.
Forceful. Compliant.
Pirouetting softly on misshapen wire hangers
as bony as ill-fed girls,
those children who eat themselves.

They face you directly
as the door closes
as quietly as your darling's thighs.

Tonight
she is your mother,
tomorrow

*(Shall I dance for you, mister?)*
she is your sister
or worse still:
your wife.

Oh. The dirt. The impossible beautiful dirt. Such pretty ugly.

She is the third person everyone speaks about,
the bit in between
the story.

Don't ask her to come dressed as herself.
That skin
she keeps clean and pressed
beneath her single bed.

She lies in bed all day. She has always lied in bed.

In the dressing room
she drapes her skeleton
in a fine skin of your selection
(something like this, perhaps?)
to bring out the blue under her eye,
the black of her cheek.

Her smile runs. Ladders like stockings.

Perhaps this one, sir?
This child,
she is you when your skin was plain paper
before all of the crossing-out,
the heavy words in a foreign language,
before the fingerprints,
before the burning,

before it was difficult to remember and harder to forget
and back still further
to when the child could not spell her name
or dial a hard number

or be still. Be. Still.

Perhaps this one, then, sir?
This embryo,
she is you when you were a thought,
a whisper between strangers.

Or even this?
This simple static woman,
this ugly,
this ordinary,
such dirt,
such exquisite filth.

Or I could dress as you, sir,
if you like,
and you can lie to yourself

all night.

**(III)**

**a hidden gender**

She once killed a man.
She once killed two,
or was it more...?
Perhaps more.
I forget.

She kills them with conversation.
Some die of disappointment
or blasted full face with double-barrelled kisses,
sawn-off blow jobs.

She casts her line
into grey rivers of fast-flowing ill-lit roads,
catching men
flapping in her fishnet tights
or staked with a red stiletto heel at the river bank.

She keeps them
un-ironed
in clumps at the corners of her bedsit.
Even her laugh is the sound of a door slamming,
an evening ending.

Sometimes –
bored perhaps –
she rifles though the piles of men
whose smiles are creases
and sometimes
one fits her.

There was one early evening
late London summer
when she dressed in a man –
though the chest pinched and the shoulders slid
as though trying to escape –
and sat in a lowered eyelid of a Soho café
sipping drinks she did not understand
and waiting for a woman
who may be eased from her skin

and worn in the warmer weather
when she caught her own eye
in the reflection of the glass rim.
Smiled once. Cleared her throat
and took herself home that evening.

# Jar of Souls

There once was a woman
who kept her soul in a jar
on the kitchen window sill,
tightly sealed
like lovers' lips,
labelled in clear print: *Dream #3*.

Listen closely.

At night
she watched the aurora borealis
of her kaleidoscope spirit
shapeshift,
diaphanous mist,
her life's drift,
phone calls missed
and that last tasteless kiss;
it tap-danced sometimes
to music she could almost remember.

This dangerous safety.
This ugly beauty.
This tan line around her heart.

There once was a woman
who kept her dreams in jars.

There once was a woman
who was a mirage.

# The Acrylic Woman

They
caught the butterfly
in gauze nets
as soft as the tatty clouds
and white sand roads,
took it home,
pinned it to parchment,
grinned
and glazed it.

He
bought the enamelled butterfly
and strung it around the neck
of the native woman he had caught
in gauze nets of dresses
as soft as the tatty promises
he made her,
took her home
and pinned her to the bed sheets,
grinned and glazed
in acrylic
insincerity
and the correct way to breathe –
and showed her to his friends.

They admired her enamelled smile.

*Ah,*
they murmured.

*Freedom*
*is a beautiful*
*thing.*

# The Dishonest Pathologist

It was a dull day –
they often are –
an English grey of unwashed dishes
and drying nappies
when he entered the cold room
and fed his hands to hungry gloves,
as latex as his smile,
that snapped and licked his fingers.

The scalpel shone as her eyes once had
and her skin lay before him
like an unexplored land.
He was Columbus. Freud. The missionary man.
Discovering worlds that were already there,
venturing bravely into the known.

He checked his watch
and began.
Cartographer,
he traced lines of latitude and longitude
in thin red smiles,
proof-marked her skin,
an imperfection here,
a correction there,
a misspelling of limbs.
It would take years for them to untangle his handwriting.

A coronary the cause, perhaps.

Women's hearts often attack them,

leap up from blind alleyways
where the shadows shine
and smother their owners,
or are used as blunt instruments by well-dressed men
with bouquets like bludgeons.

He had seen this before.

He made a note on
her hip. A foot note. Cleared his throat.

He was surprised to see the hand.

His eyebrows the arched backs of black cats.
A hand.
Pink chipped nail varnish.
Extending from her belly.
A bangle. Cheap.
The shadow of a ring
missing.
He examined it carefully,
stroked it with the blunt edge of his scalpel
and watched it curl into a comma,
a small child beneath a desk.
He unpeeled his glove,
his pale hand fluttering
too close to the flame,
and took hers in his own
and felt the tug of something like life.
Showed the blunt edge of his smile

and climbed in.

We still hear him sometimes,
his voice
the echo inside a woman.

# The Illustrated Woman

There was once a woman
as blank as this page began
who tattooed herself
with herself,
eye over eye,
fingers fitting fingers,
an ink skin superimposed above her own.
Her body was a book of flickers,
a library,
an archive,
a gallery.

Her face was slightly out of register,
a bad print job.
Even her voice was tattooed
but she learned to mime to her own words
and synchronised her smile.

The soul was difficult,
would not keep still,
streaked across the living room and up the stairs
until it was finally netted and pinned
smiling to the bed sheet
ready for the needle sting.

She was never more herself than when she was being someone else.

It is said that at night
when the moon was a bright puncture wound,
a scar across the sky,

the ink woman
would rise from her skin,
a temporal astral projection,
leaving her earthly form at home
and move through town,
the ghost of herself,
the ricochet of a laugh,
an ink print on the pillow.

Remember this:
there is more truth in artifice.
The fiction is the fact.
In fact
the fiction is the fact.

# The Orchard Keeper

This morning
an absent woman
in a white coat
with a white smile
as wide as scalpels,
as tight as hospital sheets,
raised an eyebrow,
the flag of an invader,
leaned forward
and took cuttings from
my womb.

She put the clippings
in a pot on the window sill
above her sink
that held one wine glass,
red,
tipped to the side
in a parody of last night,
and watered them with kind words,
well-fed promises
and poems from the old land.

This evening
they have grown
into a full fruiting
orchard,
the branches
pushing through the window pane
and reaching for the sun.

It is said that some of the fruit
wears my face.
It is said that the fruit of the womb tree is bitter
and bites
and that each seed
is a child.

Plant them in good soil.
They are flowers that grow toward the dark.

# A Prayer for Those Who Eat the Wings of Birds

It was a Saturday,
an old man of an afternoon,
grey and hunched
counting imaginary friends
and we had been shopping,
mother and daughter,
you
persuading me to help
with the promise of food
laid behind you like breadcrumbs.

In the Nagasaki grin of the supermarket
in the paparazzi stare of a fluorescent
that seemed to turn on the dark

we sat at plastic tables and chairs as moulded as our smiles
and watched parents feed children the wings of birds
and you said,

*I'll get you some, our kid.*

And when you finally did,
months later perhaps,
I didn't eat the wings of birds
but kept mine
alive
beneath my bed
knowing that I would one day need them.

In my pocket

are the wings of birds.

Thank you.

I need them.

# The Pregnant Man

It began with blood,
a red photograph on the bed sheets
in which he could see himself as a woman,
and when the pains began –
sharp as an own goal,
as hard as closing time –
was not surprised. Composed himself. Breathed.
Shaved his face blank
in the bathroom mirror
and beneath the scribbles of hair
he found her waiting there.

Archaeology of the body.

*There is someone else here.*
*Just beneath the dust of the skin.*
*Silent. Watching. Waiting.*

He carried the woman inside him
for eight months and counting
until finally
one eye-bag open-mouth afternoon
he burst
over the living room carpet
and the patterns chased each other up the walls
and stayed.

Never much of a man
and even worse husband.
Who would have thought that within him
was the perfect woman?

# The Cloud Collector

You kept clouds in bottles
lined up on the window ledge
so that the curtains would never quite meet.

Clear glass. Green. Blue. The unspoken parts of the rainbow.
    Colours that are hard to hear.

Sometimes
you polished them
and told tales of the undiscovered land
that would change everything
when found.

This,
you said,
was a cloud caught in a net
at the top of a mountain whose name you could not pronounce
but always you looked upward toward the light bulb,
the one you said
a child danced within,
and in your eyes
I saw small birds flutter.

This one
you stalked,
three years it took you,
with a sharp pen to hunt it down
over cracked palms of plains and canyons
as wide as children's mouths
until you had it cornered in a bar

and it slipped into the bottle it drank from.

And this,
your favourite,
was a cloud caught in the act of becoming
rain.
Inside I could see the trace of a smudged horizon
on which cattle or women grazed
and sometimes met my eye before flickering silent
and in the distance
the sound of something coming.

One night
it thundered in the bottle
and lightning coiled electric snake around its circumference.
A storm is remembering you, you said.

You are almost here.

# Higgs and Boson

Let's walk from one side of the city to another
in the thick night-breath of summer,
me on one side and you on the other.
Let's meet geographically impossibly in the centre.
Let's write poetry on pavements,
graffiti our skin in love letters.
Let's chart the sunrise
across the wild dark of each other's eyes
from a high window in Holloway
mapped with our palm prints,
silent
and together.

Let's go where words are afraid to –
let's never use words to speak –
teach me to dance;
worlds are made where we meet.
Let's go fishing in each other's eyes
and see what we catch.
Let's set it free.
Let's lie in bed awake
and jump the sapphire stepping stones of the stars.
Let's name them after our mothers.
Let's learn to dream in different languages.
Let's laugh inappropriately though bird fists
at life's ridiculous challenges.
Let's use our hearts as compasses
and as time passes
let's etch a map of the London Underground
across our faces.

Let's travel without moving.

We are anywhere.

Let's not get drunk tonight.

Let's paint smeared pictures of paradise with sticky fingers against
   the television screen.

Let's dream.

Let's turn up the central heating

and pretend we are not here anymore.

With you

anything is possible.

Let's write songs our fathers taught us.

Strange son. Adventurous daughter.

You were the face that launched a thousand texts.

So today: let's stay in bed.

Yes,

let's do something stupid,

let's forget our next breaths,

let's not expect

anything.

Let's. Go. Missing.

Let's walk where the wind goes.

Let's turn the page of our bed and write a classic.

Let's write something impossible.

Let's stretch our lips like swaying hammocks

in which the other is carried.

Let's. Get. Married.


Let's get married.


We already are.

In my back pocket I keep that third sapphire star we named

and here it is.

How simply the universe is made.

So tonight

let's forget the past and remember the future,
let's walk from one side of the city to the other,
let's meet at midnight,
Higgs and Boson,
silent exploding sapphire
somewhere
in the precise and perfect centre.

# The Girl Who Was Not Allowed to Sing

After school that day
they caught her
singing in the bathroom,
each note,
each dancing breath
a minor rebellion.

Insurgency in the suburbs.

They closed her mouth,
stapled between the loving
jaws of their fingers,
a muzzle
of warm Mondays.

Girls
should be silent,
especially
when they are speaking.

So

she climbed into the space
between walls
and sang;
she crawled under the lip
of the carpet
and sang.

She sang
beneath breath
beneath sound

and sang
in the cracks in the conversation
in the gap between people.

She sang
like other people cry

and her voice
divided the earth
and her voice
sent tremors across rippling continents
and her voice
teased oceans to rear on their hind legs
until it reached

the girl who was not allowed to dance.

And together
quietly
they changed the world.

# The Correct Spelling of My Name

You
who write revolutionary symphonies from beneath your single bed,
who type masterpieces on back-street BlackBerries that will never
be read,
you who have never listened to a single word that you have ever
said,
who stopped listening to yourself years ago at the same time your
elders did,
and you whose eyes are sniper slits, whose mouths are trenches,
you whose friends are grey skinny birds gathered around broken
park benches
pecking breadcrumbs of ice cocaine,
you whose hollow bones whistle with other songs,
you who bought the right shoes but will never belong,
you the stiff tongue, you the mistimed,
you the off-beat, you the hurricane-eyed,
you pacifist soldiers,
you small girls folded into whispering corners,
you quiet warriors, furious tomorrows,
you with scrubbed-out lips and eyes that are afraid to close,
you whose body will not fit into your prescribed clothes
irrespective of your size,
you switch skins, you survivors of the gendercide,
you counters of the abacus of stars,
you shine eyes, you exploding hearts,
you whose mouths are scars,
you healing tongues, you who understand two wrongs
will never make a writer,
you freedom fighters, you Saturday-night survivors, you long-
distance smilers,

you who found your dream but could not spell it,
who sat at the back of the class deciphering whiteboard
    hieroglyphics,
you free-styling dyslexics,
urban mystics,
council estate prophets,
who publish poems on street corners from the printing press of
    your lips,
whose eyes when cornered are a total eclipse,
you who only learned at school that you were stupid,
that your name was Could Do Better,
you who must work harder
and you who retreat to the far corners of the cave of your hood,
who learned to beatbox by following the patterns of fist against skin
through a closed bedroom door:
you are loved.
You with eyes of television static,
you who practise your heartbeat on split lips
as soft and ripped as inner sleeve lyrics,
you who stand in the shadows of the playground
muttering a hidden language,
for whom the streets are your heritage,
you who tattoo poetry against tenement buildings,
you who are afraid to ask, who never questioned
for fear of not knowing, for fear of rejection,
you who are the quiet eye of the classroom storm,
you who will wait most of your life just to be born,
you who cannot sit in the same room as yourself,
who sit beneath the bed proof-marking your body,
you who were raised in captivity,
who spit on the rusting links of your parents' economic slavery,
you rocking boy, you flickering girl
who traces a map of an undiscovered world on your inner arm

(how can they call it self-harm?),
you who seek your identity at darkened parties in the clouded
    faces of strangers,
who trace your ancestry with broken fingers,
you beautiful believers, you courageous care leavers,
you who were once lynched from a branch of your family tree,
you whose anger is hereditary,
whose smile is a flashing blade,
whose weakness is brave,
whose eyes are shallow graves
in which both your parents are buried,
you who lost your family in the supermarket,
at the check-out,
at the chill-out,
on the thin walk home,
you who is a poem
you are afraid no one will read:

believe.

You are not a mark on a piece of paper.
You are a prayer.

Remind them of the correct spelling of your name.

All you who see a difficult sun when you close eyes:
rise.

You have found your tribe.

# Acknowledgements

The spoken word scene in the UK is a loving and conscious space created by loving and conscious people. Thanks to Chill Pill, Come Rhyme with Me, Outspoken, Tongue Fu, Book Club Boutique, Jawdance, Bang Said the Gun, She Grrrowls, Polari and all of the bars and back rooms across the country.

Thanks to all the SLAMbassadors, the originals and the unfound. In particular, thanks to the new revolutionaries: Kayo Chingonyi, Jay Bernard, Anthony Anaxagorou and Megan Beech. The pen and the microphone are batons in an inter-generational relay race – keep passing them on. Write the finishing line.

Thanks to all of those who have supported me across the years, especially when I didn't deserve it – Vanessa Lee and Spin/Stir Women's Theatre Collective, the Poetry Society, Apples and Snakes, and English PEN.

To the founders of our unquiet tongues: Benjamin Zephaniah, Linton Kwesi Johnson, Joolz.

A genuine and heartfelt thank you to Clive Birnie, who is at the heart of the spoken word revolution in publishing, and to the kindness and insightfulness of the editor of this book, Harriet Evans.

To my family and to my brothers. To David, James, Daniel, Rose, Megan, Jade and Jason.

Most of all thank you to the magical Marie Seary – the source of every good thought, every good idea, every good feeling. Thank you for inspiring self-healing.

Some of these poems are commissions or have appeared in other volumes:

*Last Poet Standing* – *Wasafiri* magazine.
*No Man's Land, The Navigator* – Intawasa (Ama Press).
*To Understand the Seed Is to Understand the Forest* – Southbank Centre and Jaybird Live Literature.
*The Pregnant Man, The House of Skin, To Dissect a Smile, The Illustrated Woman, The Orchard Keeper* – The Queen's Gallery, Leonardo da Vinci exhibition.
*Higgs and Boson* – commissioned for the marriage of James and Megan Rose.